The All Colour
Hungarian
Cookbook

The All Colour Hungarian Cookbook

100 Recipes

Compiled by Judit Miklósi

Corvina

Translated by Györgyi Jakobi
Translation revised by Dick and Mary Sturgess
Photographs by Károly Hemző
Design by Simon Koppány
© Judit Miklósi
ISBN 963 13 3024 9

Write for our catalogue to:
CORVINA
Budapest 4
P.O.B. 108
Hungary – 1364

CONTENTS

SOUPS

1 Consommé with marrow-bone

800 g (1¾ lb) beef shin, blade or rib
  bone
250 g (8–9 oz) beef bones
1 good piece of marrow-bone
mixed vegetables (carrots, parsnips,
  celeriac)
1 slice each of kohlrabi, savoy
  cabbage and cauliflower
1 small onion
1 clove garlic
100 g (3½–4 oz) fine noodles
1 small tomato, 1 green pepper
1 small piece of ginger, salt
8–10 whole black peppercorns
1 cherry-pepper

Wash the beef and the bones, put into 1½–2 l (2–3½ pt) of cold water and bring to the boil. Simmer for about an hour very slowly. Then add the washed vegetables cut into the same size and the kohlrabi, the savoy cabbage, the cauliflower, the green pepper, the tomato, and the onion. Add the garlic (enclosed in a tea-infuser or muslin bag), the cherry-pepper, the peppercorns, ginger and salt to taste. Put in the marrow-bone with the open end upward and salt it separately. Simmer slowly until the meat and the vegetables are tender. Additional water should never be added. Take out and slice the meat, strain the soup, serve the vegetables on a separate plate. Accompany with noodles cooked in water flavoured with a stock-cube.

Eat the marrow while hot on toast sprinkled with salt and red pepper.

2 Újházi chicken soup

1 chicken (1½ kg [3–4 lb])
mixed vegetables (carrots, parsnips,
  celeriac)
1 large onion
1 clove garlic
1 smaller tomato
1 green pepper
50 g (2 oz) mushrooms
200 g (7 oz) cauliflower
100 g (3½–4 oz) fresh or canned
  green peas
100 g (3½–4 oz) savoy cabbage or
  Brussels sprouts
100 g (3½–4 oz) fine noodles, salt
6–8 whole black peppercorns

Clean the chicken and cut into pieces, then put on to boil in 1½–2 l (2–3½ pt) of water. Bring to the boil, add salt, put in the whole onion, the garlic and the peppercorns in a tea-infuser or muslin bag, the whole tomato and the green pepper. Add the sliced mushrooms, the green peas (if you use tinned green peas, add only before serving), the cauliflower broken into sprigs, and the Brussels sprouts or savoy cabbage cut into strips. Boil the noodles separately in water, flavoured with a stock-cube.

Serve piping hot, placing the chicken in the tureen first, covering it with the boiled noodles, then adding the soup with the vegetables. (Remove the green pepper, tomato, onion, garlic and peppercorns before serving.)

This dish was named after the actor Ede Újházi (1844–1915).

3 Goulash soup

400 g (14 oz) boneless beef
 (shoulder or shin)
500 g (18 oz) potatoes
3 tbsp lard or oil
2 medium-size onions
1 clove garlic
2 nice crisp green peppers
1 large tomato
salt
ground caraway seeds
ground black pepper
1 heaped tbsp paprika

For the *csipetke* noodles:
1 egg
about 80 g (3 oz) flour

Cut the meat into cubes. Fry the finely chopped onion in the melted fat, remove from the heat and mix with the red pepper. Put in the meat, add salt and black pepper and cook over moderate heat. Add the caraway seeds, garlic and enough water to cover, then simmer slowly until almost tender. Add the potatoes, peeled and diced, add the green peppers, cleaned and cut into rings, the tomato, skinned and chopped, and pour in 1 l (1¾ pt) of water. When the potatoes are almost done, add the *csipetke,* made as follows:

Újházi chicken soup

Goulash soup ▶

knead the egg and the flour into a stiff dough. Pinch into small, bean-sized pieces, add to the goulash and boil slowly for some minutes. If required, add more salt. Serve piping hot.

This is a typical Hungarian one-dish meal. It differs from the goulash made in a stew-pot in that the latter has more meat and less juice.

4 Giblet soup

500 g (18 oz) chicken giblets
2 tbsp cooking oil or melted butter
1 small onion
mixed vegetables (carrots and parsnips)
2 tbsp flour
salt
1 bunch of parsley

Fry the grated onion, add the chicken giblets cut into small pieces, stir, add the vegetables cut into small pieces, salt to taste, and sauté under a lid for 4–5 minutes. Sprinkle with flour, add 1 l (1¾ pt) of water and continue cooking, stirring occasionally, until tender. Sprinkle with finely chopped parsley before serving. If necessary, add more salt.

5 Bean soup with sour cream and *csipetke*

150 g (5 oz) beans
mixed vegetables (carrots, parsnips)
300 g (10–11 oz) smoked pork (with bones) or pork knuckles
1 tbsp lard or cooking oil
2 tbsp flour
1 small onion (grated)
1 clove garlic
150 ml (¼ pt) sour cream, salt

1 tbsp paprika
vinegar

For the *csipetke:*
1 egg
approx. 80 g (3 oz) flour

After soaking the beans in water for a few hours, put them, together with the meat, in 1.2 l (2 pt) of cold water and bring to the boil. When the beans and the meat are nearly cooked, add the vegetables cut lengthwise. When the beans are done, sauté the onion in the lard, add the crushed garlic, sprinkle with 2 tablespoons of flour, and when it browns, add paprika, thin with a little broth and bring to the boil. Now mix it with the soup, and bring to the boil once more. Salt carefully and only in the final stages, since smoked pork is rather salty anyway. Separate the meat from the bones, dice it and put it back into the soup. Pinch the *csipetke* into the boiling soup (see page 9). Serve with sour cream, and you may also flavour with vinegar according to taste.

6 Mushroom soup with butter noodles

250 g (8–9 oz) mushrooms
2 tbsp cooking oil or butter
3 tbsp flour
150 ml (¼ pt) sour cream
1 small onion
salt
ground black pepper
1 tsp paprika
1 bunch of parsley
1 l (1¾ pt) meat stock (made from a stock-cube)

Giblet soup ▶

Soups

For the butter noodles:
1 egg
200 g (7 oz) butter
4 tbsp flour
salt

Sauté the finely chopped onion in about 1 tsp of oil or butter, add the thinly sliced mushrooms and continue to cook. Add salt, black pepper, and sprinkle with a little paprika, pour in the stock, cover and cook until tender. Meanwhile make a roux with the remaining oil or butter and the flour. Sprinkle the parsley on top, thin with a little of the broth, bring to the boil, add to the soup and bring this to the boil again. Add the sour cream at the very end. You may cook rice or butter noodles in it, too, before adding the sour cream.

For the noodles: knead together the ingredients, leave the dough to stand for 20 minutes, then pinch it into boiling water. Bring to the boil again and cook for 2–3 minutes.

7 Potato soup with sour cream

500 g (18 oz) potatoes
2 tbsp cooking oil
1 stock-cube
2 tbsp flour
1 small onion
150 ml (¼ pt) sour cream
salt
1 tsp paprika
200 g (7 oz) of sausages or bacon rind

Put the cleaned and diced potatoes in 1 l (1¾ pt) of cold water and bring to the boil. Add the stockcube and salt. Sauté the grated onion in the oil, add the flour, cook until golden brown, sprinkle with paprika, thin with a little of the stock and bring to the boil. Mix into the soup and continue cooking until the potatoes are done. (The dish can be made more substantial by adding sausage rings or cooking bacon rind in the soup. You may also add a green pepper or a tomato.)

8 Fish soup

1 kg (2¼ lb) of fish (preferably several kinds of fish, e.g. carp, sheat-fish, sterlet)
3 large onions
1 hot green pepper
salt
1 tsp paprika
1–2 cherry-peppers (as desired)

Clean the fish and cut into 50–60 gram (2–2½ oz) slices, then salt. Place the heads, backbones and fins in 1 l (1¾ pt) of water, bring to the boil, sprinkle with paprika and simmer for about an hour. Strain the stock, pour it over the fish slices, add the fish-roes and the cherry-peppers, and boil together for 15–20 minutes by which time it will be ready to serve. Do not stir the soup while it is cooking, just shake the saucepan from time to time. On dishing up add salt if necessary. Sprinkle with the green pepper cut into rings. Serve piping hot!

Fish soup ▶

12

9 Pea soup

750 g (1½ lb) fresh green peas
1 tbsp butter
1 l (1¾ pt) of meat stock (from
* a stock-cube)*
1 tbsp sugar
2 tbsp flour
salt
1 bunch of parsley

For the noodles:
1 egg
3 tbsp flour
salt

Shell and wash the green peas, cook them in the stock. Make a light roux from the butter and the flour, mix in the finely chopped parsley, use the mixture to thicken the soup, then add salt and sugar. Beat the egg, add salt and mix in enough flour to produce a soft dough. Pinch off pieces of dough into the boiling soup.

If the green peas are very young, you can cook a few pods in the soup, but remove them before serving.

10 *Korhely* soup

300 g (10–11 oz) sour cabbage, plus
1 l (1¾ pt) of sour cabbage liquid
1 tbsp lard or cooking oil
3 tbsp flour
1 small onion
300 g (10–11 oz) smoked sausage
150 ml (½ pt) sour cream
1 tsp paprika
salt
ground black pepper

Prepare a brown roux from the lard, the flour, and the grated onion, sprinkle with paprika and dilute with the sour cabbage liquid (if too sour, you can thin it with water). Bring to the boil, add the sour cabbage, the sausage cut into rings, salt and black pepper, and continue to simmer for another 5–10 minutes. Serve piping hot, accompanied by sour cream.

This soup is especially recommended as a pick-me-up after a party the night before (as is implied by its Hungarian name).

11 *Lebbencs* soup

80 g (3 oz) smoked bacon
100 g (3½–4 oz) lebbencs or ready-
* made pasta cut into irregular*
* squares*
1 small onion
250 g (8–9 oz) potatoes
2 green peppers
1 medium-size tomato (or 1 tbsp
* tomato paste)*
1 tsp paprika
salt
ground black pepper

Dice the bacon, render it and put aside the cracklings. Sauté the finely chopped onion in the bacon fat and lightly brown the pasta in it. Remove from the heat and sprinkle with paprika according to taste, add the cleaned and diced potatoes, the green peppers cut into rings and the chopped tomato (or the tomato paste). Add 1½ l (2¼ pt) of water, salt, and black pepper, and cook until tender. Serve piping hot, garnished with the cracklings.

Lebbencs soup ▶

12 Apple soup

500 g (18 oz) apples
juice of half a lemon
100 g (3½–4 oz) sugar
100 ml (½ pt) white wine
100 ml (½ pt) double cream
2 tbsp flour
pinch of salt
2–3 cloves garlic
small piece of cinnamon

Put the peeled and diced apple into 1 l (1¾ pt) of boiling water already sweetened and flavoured with the spices, salt and lemon juice. Cook until tender. Then add the wine, cream and flour smoothly mixed together. Bring to the boil, and remove the pieces of clove and cinnamon. Serve chilled.

13 Morello cherry soup

400 g (1 lb) morello cherries
80 g (3 oz) sugar
pinch of salt
cinnamon
cloves
peel of half a lemon
2 tbsp flour
200 ml (⅓ pt) double cream
100 ml (⅕ pt) semi-sweet red wine
(to taste)

Stone the morello cherries, then put them into boiling water already sweetened, salted and flavoured with the spices and lemon peel. Bring to the boil again, simmer for 5 minutes, then add the flour and cream mixed smoothly together. Bring to boiling point again. Finally, flavour with red wine, and remove the lemon peel and spices. Serve chilled.

STARTERS

14 Casino eggs

4 hard boiled eggs
50 g (2 oz) butter
anchovy paste
100 ml (⅕ pt) sour cream
400 ml (¾ pt) tartar sauce
2 medium-size, boiled, peeled
  potatoes
salt
ground black pepper
mustard
1 bunch of parsley
1 bunch of chives
400 g (14 oz) French salad (boiled,
  diced carrots, parsnips, turnip,
  potato, raw apple, gherkins, and
  boiled green peas mixed in tartar
  sauce)

Cut the eggs lengthwise, sieve the egg yolks and the boiled potatoes while still warm, mix with the butter, add salt, mustard, black pepper, anchovy paste, sour cream and finely chopped parsley according to taste. Fill the hollows in the egg whites with the mixture, place the filled eggs on the French salad, pour the tartar sauce over the top and sprinkle with chopped chives. Serve chilled.

15 Bakony mushrooms

750 g (1½ lb) mushrooms
1 large onion
1 clove garlic
200 ml (⅓ pt) sour or double cream
2 tbsp cooking oil
2 green peppers
2 tbsp flour
salt
ground black pepper
1 tsp paprika

Wash the mushrooms well, slice them but don't peel them (to preserve their vitamin content). Sauté the grated onion in the oil, put to one side, sprinkle with paprika, add the crushed garlic, mushrooms, finely chopped green peppers, salt, black pepper, and braise the mixture in its own liquid over moderate heat. Mix the flour with the sour or double cream until smooth, add to the dish, and simmer until it achieves the consistency of a sauce. Serve immediately (reheating is not recommended).

16 Stuffed kohlrabis

8 young kohlrabis
400 g (14 oz) minced veal or pork
3 tbsp butter
1 egg
200 ml (⅓ pt) double cream
3 tbsp flour
1 roll
salt
ground black pepper
1 bunch of parsley
1 tsp sugar

Thinly peel the kohlrabis, scoop out the insides. Mix the minced meat thoroughly with the roll after soaking the latter in milk and pressing out any excess. Add the egg, salt, and black pepper, and fill the kohlrabis with this mixture. Place the kohlrabis in a buttered pan, spread their chopped leaves and scooped out insides over the top of them. If necessary, add more salt, sprinkle on a little sugar, pour in a little water, cover with a lid, bring to the boil and cook until tender. Arrange the kohlrabis on a dish, make a light roux from the remaining butter and flour, and use it to thicken the liquid remaining in the pan. Add the cream, boil the mixture well, and pour it over the kohlrabis. Sprinkle with the chopped parsley and serve piping hot.

17 Hungarian omelette

8 eggs
200 g (7 oz) veal or pork
2 medium-size onions
3 tbsp lard or cooking oil
100 ml (⅕ pt) double cream
salt
1 tsp paprika

Finely chop the onions, fry them, and remove them from the heat. Sprinkle with paprika, add the finely diced or minced meat, season with salt, and gradually adding water as necessary, continue cooking until you obtain a thick paprika sauce *(pörkölt)*. Whisk the eggs, add salt, and fry 4 omelettes in the remaining fat. Fill them with the meat and onion mixture from the strained paprika sauce. Mix the remaining hot paprika sauce with the double cream and sprinkle over the omelettes. Decorate with slices of green pepper and serve immediately while still hot.

18 Hungarian macaroni or spaghetti

60 g (2½ oz) smoked bacon
2 medium-size onions
1 clove garlic
400 g (14 oz) finely diced veal or
*   pork*
2 green peppers
1 large tomato
500 g (18 oz) macaroni
80 g (3 oz) grated Parmesan cheese
salt
2 tsp paprika

Cut the bacon into small cubes and render. Sauté the chopped onions in the resulting fat, put them aside to cool, sprinkle with paprika, add a little water and bring to the boil. Add the meat, salt, crushed garlic, diced peppers and tomato, gradually adding water as necessary to replace the liquid lost during the cooking. Continue simmering till tender. Cook the macaroni in plenty of salted water, drain and rinse and add to the dish, mixing well together. Sprinkle the grated cheese over the top and brown for a few minutes in a hot oven.

19 Fried goose liver

1 adult goose liver (400–500 g
*   [14–18 oz])*
200 g (7 oz) goose fat
1 medium-size onion
1 clove garlic
milk
salt
whole black peppercorns
paprika

Soak the liver in milk, then place in a fairly deep pan, add the fat, the peppercorns, the whole onion and the garlic. Pour on a little water, cover with a lid and stew. When the water has evaporated, brown the liver on both sides and remove from the pan. Place the liver in a fireproof dish, sprinkle it with salt and paprika according to taste, and strain the fat over it. Chill thoroughly and serve with home-made bread. Fried goose liver is also delicious served hot, sliced, accompanied by boiled potatoes sprinkled with the fat in which the liver was fried.

◄ Stuffed kohlrabis

20 Hortobágy pancakes

For the pancake batter:
2 eggs
150 g (5 oz) flour
200 ml (⅓ pt) milk
approx. 100 ml (⅕ pt) soda water
salt
oil for frying

For the filling:
400 g (14 oz) meat (pork or veal)
2 tbsp cooking oil
2 medium-size onions
200 ml (⅓ pt) sour cream
2 tbsp flour
salt
1 tsp paprika

Prepare a thick paprika sauce *(pörkölt)* from the oil, finely chopped onions, paprika and diced meat (see page 19), remove the meat from the sauce, mince or chop finely, mix together with half the sour cream and half the paprika sauce, bring to the boil and simmer for a few minutes until the sauce thickens.

Prepare a medium thick pancake batter from the ingredients given, leave to stand for at least an hour, then use it to fry thin pancakes in a little oil (there should be 8–10 of them). Fill the pancakes with the meat stuffing, roll them up and place them in a fireproof dish. Mix the remaining paprika sauce, the sour cream and the flour, bring to the boil, pour over the pancakes and heat well in the oven.

◄ Hortobágy pancakes

FISH DISHES

21 Trout stuffed with goose liver

4 medium-size trout
200 g (7 oz) goose liver
3 tbsp butter
50 ml (2 fl oz) brandy
salt
ground black pepper

Dice the goose liver, season it with salt and black pepper, marinate it in the brandy and let it stand for an hour. Clean and wash the trout, salt them well inside and out, and stuff them with the goose liver. Wrap each stuffed trout in a piece of buttered greaseproof paper. Place them in a pan and bake them in a moderate oven for about 20 minutes. Pour melted butter over them and serve with a neutral garnish, for example, mashed potatoes with cream.

22 Fried pike-perch

1–1½ kg (2¼–3 lb) pike-perch
200 ml (⅓ pt) tartar sauce
salt
1 tsp paprika
flour
oil for frying
half a lemon

Wash the pike-perch, clean it, remove the head, fillet the fish, sprinkle the fillets with salt, dip them into flour mixed with paprika and lay them in semi-circles in a pan of hot oil. Turn the fillets while frying so that both sides are nicely browned, then arrange them carefully on a plate decorated with slices of lemon. Serve with tartar sauce and fried potatoes.

23 Cold pike-perch

1 medium-size pike-perch
  (1 kg [2¼ lb])
mixed vegetables (carrots, parsnips)
1 small onion
100 ml (⅕ pt) vinegar
400 g (14 oz) French salad (see
  Casino eggs)
250 g (8–9 oz) aspic jelly
1 hard boiled egg
200 ml (7 fl oz) tartar sauce
salt
4–5 whole black peppercorns
1 bay leaf

Scrape off the scales, wash the fish, clean it well, cut off the head, remove the flesh from the bone, cut it into fillets and sprinkle with salt. Clean the vegetables and the onion, cut them into rings, put them into water, add the vinegar, the bay leaf, a little salt and a few black peppercorns. Bring to the boil, put in the fish fillets, and simmer for 20 minutes. Remove the fillets from the liquid, chill and slice them with a sharp knife, and place them on top of the French salad. Decorate with finely diced aspic jelly and slices of hard boiled egg. Serve with tartar sauce.

Fried pike-perch ▶

24 Sheat-fish with sour cream

800 g (1⅓ lb) sheat-fish
80 g (3 oz) butter
50 g (2 oz) flour
300 ml (½ pt) sour cream
salt
ground black pepper
4–5 capers

Clean and slice the sheat-fish, cut the fillets from the backbone, season them with salt and black pepper, dip them in flour and fry them in butter until light brown. Now butter a pan, carefully lay the fillets in it, mix the flour with the sour cream, pour the mixture over the fillets in the pan and slowly bring to the boil without stirring. You may flavour the sauce with capers if you wish. Sprinkle finely chopped parsley over the top and serve with a neutral garnish, for example, potatoes boiled in salty water.

25 Paprika carp with mushrooms

600 g (1⅓ lb) carp (without bones)
3 tbsp butter
1 tbsp flour
200 ml (⅓ pt) sour cream
100 ml (⅕ pt) double cream
150 g (5 oz) mushrooms
1 large onion
100 ml (⅕ pt) white wine
salt
ground black pepper
1 bunch of parsley

Clean the carp, carefully remove the flesh from the bones, cut into fairly small pieces and place them in a buttered baking pan. Sprinkle with salt, cover with finely chopped onions fried in a little butter and the cleaned, sliced mushrooms. Sprinkle with chopped parsley and black pepper, pour on the wine, cover with foil (if need be add a little water) and bake in a moderate oven until tender.

Meanwhile, mix together the flour and the sour and double cream. Remove the foil and pour the mixture over the fish. Return the dish to a hot oven to heat thoroughly. Serve at once, preferably accompanied by buttered rice.

26 Carp, Serbian style

1 carp of about 1 kg (2¼ lb)
400 g (14 oz) boiled, peeled potatoes
100 g (3½–4 oz) streaky bacon
3 tbsp fat
2 large onions
200 ml (⅓ pt) sour cream
2 large tomatoes
2 large green peppers
salt
3 tsp paprika

Grease a baking tin, arrange the sliced, boiled potatoes on the bottom, place the fish fillets on top, alternating with thin slices of bacon (set aside a few for decoration). Meanwhile sauté the finely chopped onions in the fat, season with paprika, dilute with 100 ml (⅕ pt) of water, thicken, add the peeled tomatoes and peppers, cut into small pieces, add salt and boil together. Pour the mixture over the fish in the baking tin. Mix 1 tsp paprika with the sour cream and pour it over the fish. Bake in a moderate oven for about 30–40 minutes. Fry the reserved bacon slices, arrange them on top of the dish and serve. Take particular care that the fish should not stick to the bottom of the pan.

27 Carp fried in breadcrumbs

800 g (1¾ lb) carp (without the
bones)
salt
flour, egg and breadcrumbs
oil for frying
300 ml (½ pt) tartar sauce

Wash and clean the carp. Fillet and salt it. Roll the fillets in flour, beaten egg, and breadcrumbs, and fry in plenty of hot oil until crisp. Place on a heated dish. Potatoes sprinkled with parsley go very well with it. Serve the tartar sauce in a separate bowl.

Carp fried in breadcrumbs

Beef

28 Beef stew with *galuska*

*800 g (1¾ lb) beef (thin flank or
  shin)*
2–3 tbsp lard or cooking oil
2 onions
1 clove garlic
*1 medium-size tomato (or tomato
  paste)*
2 green peppers
salt
1 tbsp paprika
ground black pepper

For the *galuska*:
200 g (7 oz) flour
2 medium-size eggs
2 tbsp cooking oil
salt

Sauté the finely chopped onion in the heated lard, add the beef cut into small pieces, brown well, remove from the stove, mix in paprika, salt and ground black pepper, add the peeled tomato cut into small pieces or the tomato paste diluted with a little water, the diced green pepper and the crushed garlic. Cover with a lid and stew at a moderate heat. Add a little water now and then if necessary, continue stewing until tender. Serve with boiled potatoes or *galuska* (small dumplings or noodles).

Pork stew is made in the same manner.

The *galuska* is made as follows: work together the flour, the eggs, a little salt and sufficient water to produce a firm dough. Boil 3 l (5 pt) salted water in a pot and nip off small pieces of the dough into the boiling water using a pastry-cutter, or a knife and a wet wooden board. Each *galuska* should be about 1½ cm long, and you should only cook a few at a time. When the *galuska*s have risen to the surface of the water, lift them out, rinse them with hot water, drain and heat them well in the oil. They should always be freshly made!

29 Peppered beef stew

*800 g (1¾ lb) beef (shin or thin
  flank)*
1 tbsp lard or cooking oil
1 medium-size onion
1 clove garlic
*400 g (14 oz) tomato paste (or fresh
  tomato)*
*150 ml (¼ pt) dry white wine (e.g.
  Riesling)*
salt
ground black pepper

Sauté the finely chopped onions in the fat, add the beef cut into strips, the crushed garlic, salt, pepper and wine, mix well, add a little water, then cover and simmer at a low heat, replacing the water as it evaporates. When the meat is half-cooked, add the tomato paste mixed with a little water. Sprinkle well with ground black pepper when ready and add salt to taste. Garnish with rice or mashed potatoes.

Tenderloin steaks, Budapest style ▶

30 Tenderloin steaks, Budapest style

*4 slices of tenderloin, 100–120
  g (3–4 oz) each*
3 tbsp cooking oil
60 g bacon
100 g (3½–4 oz) goose liver
120 g (4 oz) mushrooms
2 large onions
1 large tomato (or tomato paste)
2 large green peppers
*100 g (3½–4 oz) shelled green peas
  braised in butter*
salt, 1 tsp paprika
1 stock-cube

Brown the finely chopped onions in a small quantity of oil, add paprika, the tomato cut into small pieces, and the crumbled stock-cube, dilute with a little water, and cook for 10–15 minutes. Dice the bacon and fry until transparent, add the sliced mushrooms, the goose liver and the diced green peppers, pour on the strained paprika sauce and boil well together. Finally, add salt. Season the steaks with salt and fry them in the remaining oil—underdone or well done according to taste. Pour on the piping hot ragout, sprinkle with the braised green peas and serve at once, decorating with rings of green pepper and tomato. Accompany with steamed rice.

Beef

31 The Seven Chieftains' stew with *galuska*
(a Transylvanian speciality)

200 g (7 oz) beef steak
200 g (7 oz) pork (shoulder or thin flank)
200 g (7 oz) veal
2 tbsp lard or cooking oil
800 g (1¾ lb) smoked streaky bacon
2 large onions
2 large green peppers
1 large tomato
200 ml (⅓ pt) sour cream
1 tbsp flour
salt
1 tsp paprika

For the *tarhonya*:
250 g (8–9 oz) tarhonya *(rice-shaped noodles)*
1 medium-size tomato
1 green pepper
1 medium-size onion
2 tbsp cooking oil
salt
1 tsp paprika
1 stock-cube

Cut the meat into small cubes. Fry the diced bacon, add the finely chopped onion, sauté them, remove from the heat, sprinkle with paprika, add a little water and bring to the boil. Now put in the pork and when it is almost ready, add the veal, together with the chopped green peppers and the skinned and chopped tomato. Add water from time to time to replace the liquid as it evaporates, and finally add the sour cream smoothly mixed with the flour. Bring to the boil again and serve piping hot. Garnish with *galuska* or *tarhonya* (see pages 26, 28). Fry the *tarhonya,* stirring continuously, salt, add the whole onion, sprinkle with paprika and dilute with hot water to twice the volume of the mixture. Add the stock-cube, bring to the boil, then add the diced green pepper and the peeled and sliced tomato. Cover and place in a moderate oven, or cook at moderate heat without stirring until soft. It is important that the grains of *tarhonya* should be soft, but they should not stick to each other. Remove the onion before serving.

32 Sirloin steak with onions

4 steaks, 150–200 g (5–7 oz) each
100–150 g (4–5 oz) lard or oil
4 large onions
flour
salt
ground black pepper

Beat the steaks and nick their edges. Thinly slice and salt the onions, dip them in flour. Fry them until golden brown and put them aside to keep warm. Put the steaks into the fat in which you fried the onions after salting them, sprinkling them with ground pepper and rolling them in flour. Fry them quickly on both sides, place them on a flat dish, and cover them with the fried onions. Serve with fried potatoes (chips) and mustard.

Sirloin steak with onions ▶

33 Sirloin steak *(serpenyős)*

4 sirloin steaks, 150–200 g
(5–7 oz) each
2 tbsp lard or cooking oil
onions
3 large green peppers
2 medium-size tomatoes (or tomato
paste)
800 g (1¾ lb) potatoes
1 clove garlic
salt
1 tbsp paprika
ground black pepper
caraway seed to taste

Beat the steaks, nick their edges, salt them, roll them in flour and fry them quickly on both sides. Put them into another pan and keep them warm. Sauté the finely chopped onions, the crushed garlic and the caraway seeds in the fat in which you fried the steaks. Remove from the stove and sprinkle with paprika and ground black pepper. Stir, add a little water, then bring to the boil and pour the mixture over the steaks making sure that they are covered. Braise with the lid on the pan at a low heat. When the steaks are almost cooked, add the potatoes, peeled and sliced, the sliced green peppers, and the skinned and sliced tomatoes. Add enough water to cover. Salt again, put the lid on and cook until done.

Garnish with chilled home-pickled gherkins.

34 Smoked brisket of beef with beans

800 g (1¾ lb) smoked brisket of beef
400 g (14 oz) large white beans
50 g (2 oz) goose fat
1 large onion
2 cloves garlic
1 tbsp flour
4 eggs
salt
ground black pepper
1 tsp paprika

Soak the beans overnight and together with the goose fat, finely chopped onions, crushed garlic, paprika, ground black pepper and salt put them into a deep casserole. Add 1 l (2 pt) of water and bring to the boil, stirring occasionally. Rinse the smoked brisket of beef and add it to the beans, together with the eggs after washing them. Cover the casserole and cook in the oven for at least 3–4 hours at moderate heat. When the dish is done, take the meat out of the casserole. Cut it into slices, and lay them on top of the beans, decorating with slices of hard boiled eggs. Salt carefully since the smoked beef is already salty. This dish can also be prepared with goose legs and brisket of beef in equal proportions.

Smoked brisket of beef with beans ▶

35 Great Plain sirloin steak

*4 sirloin steaks, 150–200 g
   (5–7 oz) each
3 large onions
1 clove garlic
2 tbsp lard or cooking oil
100 g (3½–4 oz) streaky bacon
mixed vegetables (carrots and
   turnips)
3 green peppers
2–3 large tomatoes
salt
1 tsp paprika
caraway seeds*

Beat the steaks, nick their edges, salt them, roll them in flour, and fry them quickly on both sides in 1 tbsp of hot fat. Set aside. Put the finely chopped bacon into the same frying pan and when it is partially done, add the finely chopped onions and the crushed garlic. Sauté, then remove from the stove. Add salt, sprinkle with paprika, add a little water and bring to the boil. Pour over the steaks (which should still be warm), put on the lid and simmer gently. Clean and julienne the vegetables. Put them into a pan with 1 tbsp of fat, cover and braise until nearly done. Add them to the sirloin steaks (which should be almost ready by now) together with the green peppers and tomatoes cut into rings, and simmer until tender.

Serve accompanied by potatoes boiled in salt water.

Veal

36 Veal fricassé

800 g (1¾ lb) veal
mixed vegetables (carrots and
*   turnips)*
100 g (3½–4 oz) mushrooms braised
*   in butter*
100 g (1¾ lb) green peas braised in
*   butter*
2 tbsp butter
1 tbsp flour
1 small onion
100 ml (⅕ pt) double cream
salt
8–10 black peppercorns
1 bunch of parsley
a little lemon juice

Cut the meat into cubes, dice the vegetables, place together with the whole onion and the grains of black peppercorns (enclosed in a tea-infuser or muslin bag) in water enough to cover. Add salt, and simmer gently until the meat is nearly done. Prepare a light roux from 1 tbsp each of butter and flour and thin with a small quantity of cold water. Bring to the boil, add the finely chopped parsley, and mix carefully with the meat. Add the sliced mushrooms and green peas braised in butter, and boil well together. Add double cream, and flavour with lemon juice to taste. Remove the whole onion and the peppercorns before serving, and garnish with steamed rice.

37 Stuffed breast of veal

800 g (1¾ lb) breast of veal
2 white rolls
2 eggs
1 small onion
2 tbsp cooking oil
150 ml (¼ pt) milk
salt
ground black pepper
1 bunch of parsley

Wash the meat, push a knife through it length-wise to make pockets for stuffing, taking care not to split the sides. Sauté the finely chopped onion in 1 tbsp of oil, and add it to the rolls after soaking them in milk and squeezing them out. Add the eggs and the finely chopped parsley. Season with salt and ground black pepper and mix well. Stuff the breast of veal with this mixture, stitch the ends together with a needle and thread and rub salt on the meat. Place it in a baking tin and heat the remaining tbsp of oil. Pour it over the meat, then roast it in a moderate oven, basting frequently, until nicely brown.

Before carving, the meat should be left to stand for 10–15 minutes after removal from the oven, otherwise it will fall to pieces.

Serve with potatoes covered with the gravy from the pan.

38 Hungarian veal escalopes

600 g (1¼ lb) loin of veal
3 tbsp cooking oil
3 medium-size onions
800 g (1¾ lb) peeled, boiled
  potatoes, sliced
2 green peppers
2 medium-size tomatoes
flour
salt
1 tsp paprika

Fry the finely chopped onions in 1 tbsp of oil, remove from the heat, and sprinkle with the paprika. Add the sliced tomatoes and green peppers, add salt and a little water, and boil for a few minutes. Cut the meat into 300 g (10–11 oz) slices, beat them well, and salt and flour them. Heat the remaining oil thoroughly and fry the escalopes on both sides over high heat. Place the escalopes in the previously prepared sauce, cover with a lid and simmer slowly. Fry the boiled and sliced potatoes in the oil left over from frying the meat. Season with salt and serve as a garnish, hot from the pan.

Hungarian veal escalopes

39 Paprika veal

*800 g (1¾ lb) shoulder or knuckle of
  veal
1 tbsp lard or cooking oil
1 large onion
1 tbsp tomato paste
2 large green peppers
1 medium-size tomato
200 ml (⅓ pt) of double or sour
  cream
1 tsp flour
salt
1 tsp paprika*

Fry the finely chopped onions, add the meat cut into cubes and fry it too. Remove from the stove and sprinkle with paprika. Add a little water and the tomato paste and bring to the boil. Add the sliced green peppers, and the tomato skinned and diced. Salt, cover with a lid and simmer. Stir occasionally adding a little water if necessary. When the meat is done, thicken with the double or sour cream mixed with the flour, but be careful not to let the mixture burn. Garnish with *galuska* (see page 26) or steamed rice.

40 Calves' feet with mushrooms and sour cream

*2 calves' feet (for 4 persons)
2 tbsp cooking oil
200 g (7 oz) mushrooms
100 ml (⅕ pt) sour cream
1 tsp flour
salt
ground black pepper*

Wash and salt the calves' feet, and place them in a baking tin with a lid. Pour on hot oil and bake in a moderate oven, basting them with their own gravy. Replace the liquid with water as necessary. When the calves' feet are tender, add the thoroughly washed and sliced mushrooms, cover and replace in the oven for another 5 minutes. Mix the flour with the sour cream and pour the mixture over the calves' feet. Bring to the boil, adding salt and black pepper to taste. Serve with steamed rice.

Pork

41 Transylvanian mixed grill on wooden plate

4 pork cutlets, 50 g (2 oz) each
4 beef steaks (fillet steaks if possible), 50 g (2 oz) each
4 slices of veal, 50 g (2 oz) each
4 slices of veal liver, 50 g (2 oz) each
4 tbsp oil for frying
80 g (3 oz) smoked bacon
800 g (1¾ lb) potatoes, boiled in their jackets, peeled and sliced
flour
salt
ground black pepper
mixed salad (cucumber, lettuce, cabbage, etc.)

This is a speciality which is always to be found on restaurant menus.

Fry the meat immediately before serving, after seasoning it with salt and ground black pepper, and dipping it in flour. The liver should only be salted after frying, when you are ready to serve it, and the beef should only be salted just before frying. Cut the bacon into 4 slices, nick the rind, fry and place on top of the meat. Fry the sliced potatoes in the fat used for frying the meat. Arrange the freshly cooked meat on top of the freshly fried potatoes on a round wooden plate. Decorate with mixed salad.

42 Temesvár pork cutlets

4 pork cutlets, 120 g (4 oz) each
100 g (3½–4 oz) streaky bacon
2 medium-size onions
1 clove garlic
3 tbsp cooking oil
400 g (14 oz) potatoes
250 g (8–9 oz) green beans
200 ml (⅓ pt) sour cream
1 tsp flour
salt
1 tsp paprika
1 bunch of parsley

Flatten the cutlets, salt them and roll them in flour. Fry on both sides, then remove from the pan. Fry the finely chopped onion in the oil remaining in the pan, remove from heat, and sprinkle with paprika. Add the crushed garlic and pour on a little water. Now add the peeled and thinly sliced potatoes, salt, and bring to the boil. Lay the cutlets on top, cover and braise until tender, always replacing any evaporated liquid with water as necessary. When the cutlets are nearly done, pour the flour mixed well with sour cream over them. Cut the bacon into four slices, notch the streaky edge of each slice and fry until crisp (this makes the so-called "cock's comb"). In another pan boil the green beans in lightly

Temesvár pork cutlets ▶

salted water, straining them when done. When serving, use the potatoes to form the bottom layer of the dish, place the cutlets on top, cover each of them with a mound of green beans, then pour on the paprika sauce. Sprinkle with the finely chopped parsley, and place a "cock's comb" on top of each cutlet.

43 Braised pork slices, Hungarian style

600 g (1¼ lb) loin of pork
3 tbsp lard or cooking oil
flour
2 medium-size onions
800 g (1¾ lb) potatoes, boiled in
*   their skins and peeled after boiling*
2 large green peppers
1 large tomato
salt
ground black pepper
1 tsp paprika

Cut the meat into slices, 130–150 g (4–5 oz) each. Flatten them slightly, salt, roll them in flour and fry in hot fat on both sides until golden brown. Remove them from the pan. Fry the finely chopped onions in the remaining fat, also fry the green peppers cut into rings and the skinned and sliced tomato. Add the sliced potatoes, and the meat. Shake well together and cook over fierce heat. Now (not before!) add the paprika, season with salt and ground black pepper, and stew until tender. Serve hot, accompanied by home-pickled gherkins.

44 'Csikós' *tokány*

800 g (1¾ lb) hand of pork
100 g (3½–4 oz) smoked streaky
*   bacon*
3 medium-size onions
1 tsp flour
1 tbsp tomato paste
200 ml (⅓ pt) sour cream
salt
1 tsp paprika

Cut the bacon into strips and fry. Add the finely chopped onions, fry until golden brown, then add the meat, also cut into strips. Remove from the heat and sprinkle with paprika. Add a little water and bring to the boil. Now add the tomato paste, salt, cover and simmer until tender. Add water as necessary to make up for liquid lost during the cooking. Mix the flour with the sour cream and pour over the meat. Boil for a few minutes, and serve hot.

Garnish with *galuska* (see page 26) or *tarhonya*

45 Pork cutlets in paprika and tomato *(lecsó)*

4 pork cutlets, 120 g (4 oz) each
3 tbsp lard or cooking oil
2 medium-size onions
2 cloves garlic
80 g (3 oz) streaky smoked bacon
4 green peppers
3 large fresh tomatoes
salt
1 tsp paprika
marjoram

Flatten and salt the cutlets, fry until half-done, then place in another pan. Fry the finely chopped onions and the crushed garlic in the remaining fat until golden brown. Add a little water, sprinkle with paprika and bring to the boil, then pour over the cutlets and cook slowly. Meanwhile, cut the bacon into strips and fry in another pan. Add the sliced green peppers and the skinned and sliced tomatoes. Sprinkle with salt, cover the pan and cook at a moderate heat for a few minutes, then add to the cutlets, cover with a lid and continue cooking until all the ingredients are done. Serve with *tarhonya* (see page 28) or peeled potatoes boiled in salty water.

Braised pork slices, Hungarian style

46 Robbers' kebabs

150 g (5 oz) pork (tenderloin or chops)
150 g (5 oz) veal
150 g (5 oz) beef steak
150 g (5 oz) veal or pork liver
150 g (5 oz) smoked bacon
1 tbsp cooking oil
4 smallish onions
8 mushrooms
salt
ground black pepper
Seasons salad

Cut the bacon, the meat and the liver into equal pieces, each 4–5 cm in diameter and 3–5 cm thick. Slice the onions and cut off the stalks of the mushrooms. Divide the ingredients into 4 equal parts and thread them onto skewers, arranging them so that a slice of onion separates each piece of meat, liver, mushroom or bacon from its neighbour. Season with salt and black pepper, pour hot oil over them and grill until crisp. (They can also be fried using plenty of hot cooking oil.) Serve with salad in season and chips.

47 Crisp roasted suckling pig
(for 8–10 persons)

3–3½ kg (6–7 lb) suckling pig
lard
beer
40–50 g (1½–2 oz) bacon
salt
marjoram

If possible buy a pig just one month old. Wash well inside and out and score both sides of the backbone with a knife. Rub the inside with salt and marjoram, lay the pig in an enamelled baking tin and smear the outside evenly with cold lard or oil. Pour a little water underneath, and then place in a medium hot oven. During the cooking, rub the pig over occasionally with the bacon dipped in beer, to give it a nice colour. Wrap grease-proof paper around its ears and tail to prevent them from burning. Before serving, cut off the head, cut the pig in two lengthwise, and then into pieces. Garnish with braised cabbage (see page 50) and mashed potatoes.

This dish is suitable for New Year and other special occasions.

48 Stuffed green peppers

For the tomato sauce:
1 kg (2¼ lb) fresh tomatoes or 250 g (8–9 oz) tomato paste
2 tbsp cooking oil
3 tbsp flour
a few celery leaves
1 stock-cube
sugar
salt

For the stuffing:
80 g (3 oz) rice
1 medium-size onion
1 clove garlic
1 tbsp cooking oil
400 g (14 oz) minced shoulder of pork
1 egg
salt
ground black pepper
8 yellow-skinned, regular shaped peppers

Wash and core the peppers. Parboil the rice in fiercely boiling salt water and drain. Salt the meat and season with ground black pepper. Add the finely chopped fried onions, then the rice, the egg, and the crushed garlic. Knead well together, stuff the peppers with the mixture (but not too firmly), and make the leftover stuffing (if any) into small dumplings.

Make a light roux from the oil and the flour. Dilute with 800 ml (1 pt) of water, crumble in the stock-cube and bring to the boil. Add the tomato paste (or the tomatoes, after washing and cooking them in a little water, and passing them through a sieve) and the celery leaves also. Season with salt, then add sugar to taste.

Stuffed green peppers ▶

Place the stuffed peppers and the dumplings in the tomato sauce and cook slowly until done (do not stir, just shake the pan). Finally, remove the celery leaves and serve with potatoes boiled in salt water.

49 Transylvanian goulash

*800 g (1¾ lb) shoulder or loin of
   pork cut into 3 cm cubes
1 large onion
1 clove garlic
3 tbsp lard or cooking oil
80 g (3 oz) sour cabbage
1 tsp flour
200 ml (⅓ pt) sour cream
salt
1 tsp paprika
caraway seeds (according to taste)*

Salt the cubes of meat and roll them in the flour. Brown quickly in the lard, remove them and in the same lard fry the finely chopped onion. Remove from heat, sprinkle on paprika, add the crushed garlic and the caraway seeds. Adding a little water, bring to the boil and pour the mixture over the meat. Simmer until half-done. Now add the sour cabbage (if too sour, rinse it in water) and simmer until tender, occasionally adding a little water. When all the ingredients are tender, add the flour mixed with the sour cream and boil together. This dish can also be prepared with pork knuckles. Reheated it is even tastier.

50 Kolozsvár stuffed cabbage

*250 g (8–9 oz) minced pork
4 pork cutlets, 40 g (1½ oz) each
200 g (7 oz) smoked sausage
100 g (3½–4 oz) smoked bacon
   (50 g for the decoration)
150 g (5 oz) smoked streaky bacon
800 g (1¾ lb) sour cabbage plus
   4 whole sour cabbage leaves
2 tbsp lard or cooking oil
2 medium-size onions
1 clove garlic
1 egg
80 g (3 oz) parboiled rice
300 ml (½ pt) sour cream
2 tsp flour
salt
ground black pepper
1 tsp paprika
marjoram*

This is a rather rich, filling dish usually eaten over holiday periods. It is worth making a fairly large quantity of it since it tastes even better reheated.

Mix the minced meat with half of the finely chopped fried onions, the cooled, parboiled rice, the egg and the crushed garlic. Cut out the hard ribs of the cabbage leaves, heap the stuffing evenly on to them, fold their edges over the stuffing, and roll them up tightly. Finely dice the smoked bacon, fry it and mix it with the remaining fried onion. Place in a fairly large pan and top with one third of the rinsed sour cabbage (if too sour, soak in water for a while). Sprinkle with marjoram, paprika, salt, and ground black pepper, and lay the stuffed leaves on top. Add strips of streaky bacon and the sliced sausage. Cover with the remaining sour cabbage

Kolozsvár stuffed cabbage ▶

and add enough water to cover. Put on a lid and simmer for about an hour and a half. Mix the sour cream with the flour and take the stuffed leaves out of the pan. Add the mixture, then replace the stuffed leaves and boil together. Salt and flatten the cutlets and fry them on both sides in a separate pan. Serve with the stuffed cabbage leaves in the centre and the cutlets on top. Sprinkle any remaining sour cream over the dish, and if you like, you can decorate with "cock's combs", that is, strips of smoked bacon, notched and fried.

51 Roast pork stuffed with smoked sausage

1 kg (2¼ lb) loin of pork (in one piece)
2 tbsp lard or cooking oil
smoked sausage—the same length as your joint of pork
salt
caraway seeds
marjoram (according to taste)

Bone the meat, pierce it through the centre and stuff it with the sausage. Season with the salt and the spices. Now pour on hot fat and a little water, cover and place in a warm oven. Roast at low heat until tender. Baste frequently to make the joint crisp on the outside. Finally, take off the lid and roast in a hot oven until golden brown. Serve with steamed cabbage (see page 51) or fried potatoes.

52 Bácska pilaff

500 g (1 lb 2 oz) shoulder of pork
250 g (9 oz) rice
3 tbsp cooking oil
1 medium-size onion
2 green peppers
2 tomatoes
1 tbsp paprika

Wash and dice the meat. Finely chop the onion and fry in the oil until golden. Stir in the paprika and pour in a little water. Boil briefly, then add the meat and cook until almost tender. If necessary, replace any water which evaporates during cooking. Wash the rice, add it to the meat, together with the sliced green peppers and tomatoes. Now add water to cover, season with salt and cook slowly, stirring occasionally, until all the ingredients are tender.

Mutton and Lamb

53 Braised leg of mutton with garlic

1 kg (2¼ lb) leg of mutton
3 tbsp lard or cooking oil
mixed vegetables (carrots and
turnips)
1 medium-size onion
3–4 cloves garlic
1 tbsp tomato paste (or one medium-
size tomato)
200 ml (⅓ pt) white wine
1 tsp sugar
1 tsp flour
salt
ground black pepper
thyme
1 bayleaf

Wash and salt the meat, rub with the garlic and brown on all sides. Remove it from the pan and heat the sugar until golden. Add the mixed vegetables and the sliced onion, brown a little and sprinkle with flour. Stir, and continue browning. Season with the spices and add the tomato paste mixed with the wine. Now pour in a little water, and bring to the boil. Pour the mixture over the meat, cover with a lid and simmer, adding water as necessary, to replace liquid lost during the cooking. Scrape the bottom of the pan frequently to prevent the flour catching. When serving, strain the gravy over the top of the meat. Garnish with steamed rice or mashed potatoes.

54 Transylvanian lamb cutlets with *tarhonya*

8 lamb cutlets
2 large onions
2 tbsp lard or cooking oil
2 cloves garlic
3 medium-size tomatoes (or 2 tbsp
tomato paste)
salt
1 tbsp paprika
300 g (10–11 oz) cooked tarhonya
(see page 28)

Flatten and salt the cutlets. Fry them in hot lard on both sides, and place them in another pan. In the same lard sauté the finely chopped onions and the skinned and sliced tomatoes (or tomato paste). Sprinkle them with paprika, add the crushed garlic, a little water and bring to the boil. Pour the mixture over the cutlets, cover with a lid and simmer until tender. When serving, heap the *tarhonya* in the centre of the plate, surround it with the cutlets, and pour the sauce over the top.

55 Lamb in paprika sauce

1 kg (2–2¼ lb) lamb (shoulder or breast)
1 medium-size onion
1 clove garlic
3 tbsp lard or cooking oil
1 green pepper
1 medium-size tomato
1 tsp flour
200 ml (⅓ pt) sour cream
salt
1 tbsp paprika

Fry the finely chopped onions in the lard until golden, then remove from the heat and sprinkle with paprika. Add the meat cut into large cubes, season with salt, and fry lightly at moderate heat. Now pour on a little water, stir, and stew slowly, replacing lost water as necessary. Meanwhile, add the sliced peppers and the tomato, skinned and sliced. When the meat is tender, mix the flour with the sour cream, add and bring to the boil. Serve with potatoes boiled in salt water.

◄ Lamb in paprika sauce

56 Paprika chicken

1 chicken, about 1½ kg (2½–3 lb)
1 large onion
1 tbsp lard or cooking oil
200 ml (⅓ pt) sour cream
1 tbsp flour
1 tbsp paprika
1 small tomato (or tomato paste)
1 green pepper, salt

Fry the finely chopped onions, remove from heat and sprinkle with paprika. Add the chicken cut into portions, the salt and the slices of skinned tomato and green pepper. Cover with a lid and stew over moderate heat, adding a little water from time to time. When the meat is tender add the flour mixed with the sour cream, bring to the boil and simmer

Paprika chicken

48

until the gravy thickens to a creamy consistency. Serve accompanied by *galuska* (see page 26).

57 Fried chicken

*4 small chicken breasts or 8 small
legs
flour, egg and breadcrumbs for the
coating
plenty of oil for frying*

Salt the pieces of chicken and leave them to stand for half an hour. Wipe with a clean cloth, dip in flour, beaten egg and breadcrumbs. Deep-fry in the oil on both sides, at low heat, frying the first side with a lid on the pan and the second side without the lid. Serve accompanied by lettuce and by potatoes sprinkled with chopped parsley.

58 Fried goose liver slices

*500 g (18 oz) goose liver
flour, egg, and breadcrumbs for
coating
plenty of oil for frying
salt*

Salt the thin slices of goose liver, dip in flour, beaten egg and breadcrumbs, then deep-fry until crisp on both sides (they should not get too dry during the frying). Serve with potatoes tossed in a little fat and plenty of home-pickled gherkins and so on.

59 Gödöllő stuffed chicken

*1 chicken, about 1½ kg (2½–3 lb)
2 white rolls
3 tbsp butter
100 g (3½–4 oz) chicken liver braised
in butter
100 g (3½–4 oz) mushrooms braised
in butter
1 egg
200 ml (⅓ pt) milk
salt
ground black pepper
marjoram
1 bunch of parsley*

Soak the rolls in the milk, then squeeze them out well. Mix them together with the egg yolks, the finely chopped mushrooms and liver braised in a little butter, the parsley and the whisked egg white. Season the mixture with salt and ground black pepper. Allow it to cool, then stuff the chicken under the skin of the breast, taking care not to tear it. Sprinkle the stomach cavity of the chicken with marjoram. Put the remaining stuffing into it, then sew up the slit. Rub the chicken with salt and butter, place it in a greased baking tin, cover the breast with thin slices of bacon, and roast in a moderate oven. Serve with chips. It is a rather filling dish.

60 Roast duck or goose with red cabbage

1 duck of 2½–3 kg (6–7 lb) or goose
legs and back
2 tbsp lard
salt
marjoram

For the braised cabbage:
1 whole red cabbage
3 tbsp cooking oil
1–2 tbsp sugar
100 ml (⅕ pt) white wine according
to taste, salt, caraway seeds

Wash the duck or goose both inside and outside. Wipe with a cloth, salt inside and outside and sprinkle the inside with marjoram. Heat the lard and pour it on to the meat. Place in a medium hot oven, cover with a lid and bake, basting frequently, until tender. Now take off the lid and roast quickly until crisp and golden (all this takes about 1½–2 hours). Serve the duck with the carved breast uppermost, accompanied by braised red cabbage and/or fried potatoes.

Braise the cabbage in the following way: wash and shred the cabbage, salt, allow to stand for half an hour, then drain. Heat the

◄ Gödöllő stuffed chicken

Roast duck with red cabbage

sugar in the oil until light brown and add the cabbage. Sprinkle with caraway seeds and braise until tender, stirring gently. Replace any cooking liquid which boils away with water or wine. The cabbage should end up slightly crisp rather than soft. You can flavour it with a little vinegar too, if you wish.

61 Minced goose breast

1 goose breast including the bones
* (approx. 800 g [1¾ lb])*
1 egg
1 white roll
1 tbsp goose fat
1 tbsp cooking oil
1 clove garlic
1 small onion
salt
black pepper

Remove the meat from the bones and mince, together with the roll previously soaked in water and squeezed out. Add the egg, the finely chopped or grated onion, the crushed garlic and the goose fat, and mix well. Season the mixture with salt and ground black pepper and spread it over the breast bone. Place it in a baking tin, pour on hot oil and about 50 ml (2 fl oz) of water, cover with foil and cook in a moderate oven for about 20 minutes. Remove the foil, and continue cooking for 15 minutes, basting frequently until nicely brown.

Garnish with mashed potatoes and lettuce.

62 Roast turkey with chestnut stuffing
(for 8 persons)

1 young medium-size turkey of 3–4
* kg (6–8 lb)*
400 g (14 oz) minced pork
* (shoulder)*
800 g (1¾ lb) chestnuts
2 eggs
2 tbsp butter
200 ml (⅓ pt) double cream
1 stock-cube
salt
ground black pepper

Clean the breast cavity of the turkey with the aid of a sharp knife. Slit the chestnuts, roast in a hot oven for 15 minutes, then peel. Put the chestnuts into a pan, add a little butter and stock made from the stock-cube, cook until tender, then mash. Season the minced pork with salt and ground black pepper and moisten with the cream and the eggs. Knead well together, and add the chestnuts. Salt the inside of the turkey and fill it with the stuffing. Sew up the slit, and salt the turkey also on the outside. Place it in a baking tin, pour on the remaining hot butter and put it into a moderate oven. Baste, cover and cook until tender. Now take off the lid and roast quickly until the outside is crisp. You should reckon on one hour's cooking time per kilogram (2 lb). When done, wait a few minutes before carving, as it will fall apart if carved too hot. This is a filling dish, suitable for special occasions.

Roast turkey with chestnut stuffing ▶

63 Potatoes in sour cream sauce

1 kg (2–2¼ lb) potatoes
2 tbsp cooking oil
1 tbsp flour
100 ml (⅕ pt) sour cream
1 medium-size onion
1 tsp vinegar
salt
bayleaf
ground black pepper

Peel and slice the potatoes. Put them into a saucepan, add salt, the bayleaf and water to cover. Bring to the boil, and cook until done. Make a light brown roux, add the finely chopped onions and thin with some of the liquid drained from the potatoes. Stir until smooth, bring to the boil and pour over the potatoes. Flavour with sugar, vinegar and black pepper. Before serving remove the bayleaf, add the sour cream and bring to the boil.

64 Sorrel with sour cream

1 kg (2¼ lb) sorrel
2 tbsp butter
3 tbsp flour
200 ml (⅓ pt) milk
200 ml (⅓ pt) sour cream
salt
sugar

Remove the stalks, wash and drain the sorrel. Put into a pan and braise in butter under a lid. Add salt, sprinkle with flour and con-tinue braising for another 1–2 minutes. Thin with the milk and simmer, stirring continu-ously, at a moderate heat for about 5 minu-tes. If too thick, thin with stock or more milk. Put into a mixer with the sour cream, or pass through a sieve, then bring to the boil again and add sugar to taste.

65 Spinach purée

1 kg (2¼ lb) spinach
1 tbsp butter
2 tbsp flour
2–300 ml (7–8 fl oz) milk
1 clove garlic
200–300 ml (7–8 fl oz) stock from
*   stock-cube*
salt

Cut off the stalks, wash and drain the spin-ach. Place in salted boiling water, cook, drain and put through a sieve or purée in a mixer. Make a light roux from the butter and the flour, then add the crushed garlic and the spinach. Thin with the milk and the stock. Add salt to taste and simmer at moderate heat for about 5 minutes.

Spinach purée ▶

66 Mixed vegetables, Hungarian style

1 kg (2¼ lb) mixed vegetables
(carrots, turnips, parsnips, green peas
*   and French beans)*
2 tbsp cooking oil
1 tbsp flour
1 tsp sugar
100–200 ml (4–7 oz) milk
salt
1 bunch of parsley

Clean and dice the vegetables and sauté in oil. Season with salt, sprinkle with flour and continue sautéing for 1–2 minutes, stirring continuously. Add the finely chopped parsley, thin with cold water or milk and bring to the boil. Add more salt, stir carefully from time to time and braise until tender. Finally, add sugar to taste.

67 Paprika potatoes

1 kg (2–2¼ lb) potatoes
2–3 tbsp lard or cooking oil
2 medium-size onions
200 g (7 oz) frankfurters or other
*   sausages*
2 cloves garlic
1 green pepper
1 medium-size tomato
2 tsp paprika
salt

Fry the finely chopped onions in the fat until golden brown, remove from the heat, mix in the paprika, add the peeled, sliced raw potatoes, stir well and add water almost to cover. Salt, and add the crushed garlic, the finely chopped green pepper and the sliced tomato. Cover with a lid and stew gently, shaking occasionally, until tender. Finally, add the sliced frankfurters or other sausages and continue cooking until all the ingredients are done. Serve accompanied by home-pickled gherkins. This is a typical Hungarian one-dish meal.

68 *Lecsó*

1 kg (2–2¼ lb) fresh green peppers
500 g (18 oz) tomatoes
3 large onions
100 g (3½–4 oz) smoked bacon
1 tbsp cooking oil
salt
1 tbsp paprika

Finely dice the bacon. Heat the oil in a fairly large pan and fry the diced bacon and the onion cut into semicircular slices until light brown. Remove from heat, mix in the paprika, add the sliced peppers and return the pan to the heat. After 5 minutes add the skinned and sliced tomatoes, and salt carefully (the bacon will be salty too). Cook first over high heat without a lid. Then, before the liquid has boiled away, put the lid on and continue cooking over moderate heat until done.

If the *lecsó* is served as a separate course, frankfurters or other sausages may also be cooked in it. Another option is to add beaten eggs immediately before serving to make it richer.

Lecsó ▶

69 Vegetable marrow with sour cream

1 kg (2¼ lb) shredded marrow
1 tbsp cooking oil
2 tbsp flour
vinegar
200 ml (7 oz) double or sour cream
1 large bunch of fresh dill
salt
sugar

Put the shredded marrow into hot oil. Add salt and a little vinegar. Cover with a lid and braise, stirring occasionally, until nearly tender. Then add the flour mixed with the double or sour cream. Add sugar to taste, and bring to the boil. This is a delicious dish either hot or cold but take care not to overcook the marrow.

70 French beans with sour cream

1 kg (2¼ lb) French beans
2 tbsp cooking oil
1 tbsp flour
1 small onion
1 clove garlic
vinegar
200 ml (7 oz) sour cream
paprika
sugar
1 bunch of parsley

String and wash the beans, cut them into fairly small pieces. Put them into slightly salted boiling water, cook until tender, then drain, reserving the liquid. Fry the finely chopped onions, add the flour and continue browning. Add the crushed garlic, and remove from heat. Sprinkle with paprika, thin with the liquid in which the beans were cooked, bring to the boil, and pour the mixture over the French beans. Bring to the boil again, add sugar and a few drops of vinegar to taste, sprinkle with chopped parsley, add the sour cream and bring to the boil once more.

71 Lentils, Hungarian style

400 g (14 oz) lentils
1 piece of smoked bacon rind
2 tbsp cooking oil
1 tbsp flour
1 medium-size onion
1 clove garlic
lemon juice
200 ml (⅓ pt) sour cream
1 tsp sugar
1 tbsp mustard
vinegar
1 pinch of paprika
1 bayleaf
salt

Rinse the lentils and soak them in cold water overnight. Put them on to cook in fresh cold water. Add the bacon rind and the bayleaf. Season with salt, cover with a lid and simmer until soft. Fry the finely chopped onion and the garlic, add the flour, and continue frying until light brown. Now sprinkle with the paprika. Thin with a little cold water and bring to the boil. Pour on to the cooked lentils and flavour with vinegar, sugar, mustard, and lemon juice, according to taste. Finally, add half the sour cream, bring to the boil again, and sprinkle with the remaining sour cream before serving.

Lentils, Hungarian style ▶

72 Savoy cabbage in sauce

800 g (1¾ lb) savoy cabbage
400 g (14 oz) potatoes
2 tbsp cooking oil
1 heaped tbsp flour
1 medium-size onion
1 clove garlic
salt
ground black pepper
1 tsp paprika
ground caraway seeds or marjoram

Wash and shred the savoy cabbage. Sprinkle it with salt, and place it in a little fiercely boiling, lightly salt water. Add the caraway seeds or the marjoram, cover and continue boiling over moderate heat. When half-done add the peeled, diced potatoes. Meanwhile, fry the finely chopped onion, add the flour and continue frying until light brown. Add the black pepper, the crushed garlic and the paprika. Thin the resulting roux with cold water, before bringing it to the boil and pouring it over the savoy cabbage. Bring to the boil once more. If the cabbage is too watery, pour some of the water off before adding the roux.

Savoy cabbage in sauce

SALADS

73 Home-pickled gherkins

1 kg (2¼ lb) gherkins (medium-size)
1 slice of bread
50 g (2 oz) salt
2 l (3½ pt) water
1 clove garlic
1 bunch of dill
2–3 black peppercorns
1 bayleaf

Salt the water and bring to the boil. Meanwhile, cut off the ends of the gherkins and check to make sure that they do not taste bitter. Place the dill at the bottom of a large preserving jar, put in the gherkins, standing upright. Add the garlic, the bayleaf, the peppercorns and the slice of bread, and pour on warm salted water to cover. Cover the jar with a cheesecloth and leave it to stand in a sunny place for 4–5 days to allow the contents to ferment. When the process is complete, place the cucumbers in another jar, pour the strained liquid over them, and store in a cool place. Serve chilled, and peeled if you wish.

74 Potato salad

750 g (1½ lb) boiled potatoes
1 large onion
salt
sugar
ground black pepper
1 tbsp salad oil
mild vinegar

Boil the potatoes in their skins, peel and cut them into thin rounds. Cut the onion into rings and place them, together with the potato rounds, into a dressing made of salt, vinegar, ground black pepper and sugar. Leave the salad to stand for at least a day, and mix in the oil just before serving.

75 Green pepper salad

8 green peppers
vinegar
sugar
salt
1 tbsp salad oil

Wash and core the peppers and cut them into rings. Scald with boiling salted water, drain and pour on a dressing of vinegar, salt and sugar, blended according to taste. Prepare the salad 2–3 hours before it is required, chill it, and mix in the oil just before serving.

76 Tomato salad

750 g (1½ lb) firm, ripe tomatoes
wine vinegar
salt
sugar
salad oil
ground black pepper
1 bunch of parsley
1 small onion

Wash the tomatoes, skin them if you wish, and cut them into rings. Place them in a dish, pour on a dressing made of salt, sugar, ground pepper, vinegar, oil and finely chopped onions. Chill, and serve with parsley sprinkled on top.

◄ Tomato salad

77 Cucumber salad with sour cream

750 g (1½ lb) cucumber
2 cloves garlic
mild vinegar
sugar
1 tbsp cooking oil
sour cream
salt
ground black pepper
pinch of paprika

Slice the peeled cucumber, salt it, let it stand, squeeze it out gently, then pour on a dressing of mild vinegar, sugar and crushed garlic. Leave to stand for half an hour, then

Cucumber salad with sour cream

remove from the dressing, mix with the oil, pour on the sour cream and serve chilled, sprinkled with red pepper and ground black pepper.

78 Cabbage salad

1 cabbage—approx. 1 kg (2¼ lb)
salt
vinegar
sugar
caraway seeds
salad oil

Wash and shred the cabbage, scald it with boiling salted water, then drain. When cool, toss in a dressing made of salt, vinegar, sugar and caraway seeds. Sprinkle with a little oil before serving, if you wish.

79 Gellért salad

1 kg (2¼ lb) beetroot
vinegar
20–30 g (¾–1 oz) horseradish
sugar
lemon juice
300 ml (½ pt) mayonnaise sauce
French mustard
salt
caraway seeds
cayenne pepper
lettuce and parsley for decoration

This is the creation of Károly Gundel, a famous cook of the early part of this century, who was also the chef of the Budapest Gellért Hotel.

Wash and cook the beetroots in their skins in plenty of water. When tender, peel and slice them thinly. Make a dressing from half a litre (1 pt) of water, salt, vinegar, sugar, caraway seeds and horseradish and let the beetroot stand in it for a day. Drain and cut the beetroot slices into strips. Immediately before serving stir the strips into mayonnaise seasoned with cayenne pepper, lemon juice and mustard. Decorate the edge of the dish with lettuce and sprinkle parsley on top.

PASTAS, CAKES, AND DESSERTS

80 Pasta with cabbage

400 g (14 oz) flour
1 large egg (or two small ones)
1 kg (2–2¼ lb) cabbage
3 tbsp cooking oil
salt
ground black pepper
sugar

You can use the pasta which is available ready made in the shops. If you prepare the pasta yourself, first mix the flour with the eggs, a little salt, and some lukewarm water, then knead into a stiff dough. Shape into two lumps. Roll each lump out thin, let them dry a little, then cut them into about 1 cm (half-inch) squares. Shred the cabbage, salt and, after a few minutes, squeeze out the moisture. Heat the oil, put the cabbage in it together with the sugar and fry. Cook the squares of dough in boiling salted water. Rinse them under hot water, drain, and add to the cabbage. Season to taste with ground black pepper and serve hot.

81 Jam pockets

400 g (14 oz) flour
4 eggs
50 g (2 oz) butter
80 g (3 oz) castor sugar
100 g (3½–4 oz) breadcrumbs
250 g (8–9 oz) plum or apricot jam
cinnamon
salt

Make a dough with the flour, three eggs, a pinch of salt and a little water. Shape into two lumps, roll each one out thin. On one half of the dough place small heaps of jam about 3 cm apart, smear the spaces between them with beaten egg, carefully cover with the other half of the dough, pressing the places between the heaps of jam gently down with your fingers and cut into squares with a pastry cutter. Press the edges of the squares together once more to prevent the jam leaking out. Cook in boiling salted water, drain and roll in the breadcrumbs lightly browned in the butter and mixed with castor sugar and cinnamon. Serve hot.

82 Jam-filled buns

300 g (10–11 oz) flour
100 ml (4 fl oz) milk
20g (¾ oz) yeast
2 eggs (one for brushing over)
4 tbsp butter or margarine
approx. 200 g (7 oz) plum jam
salt
2 tbsp sugar

Mix the yeast with 1 tsp sugar and lukewarm milk and leave it to rise. Now add it to the flour, together with the rest of the sugar, a pinch of salt, the egg, and a quantity of lukewarm milk to produce a medium-stiff dough. Knead well. Slowly add 2 tbsp melted butter and continue kneading. Place on a board dusted with flour, or in a bowl. Cover with a clean cloth, and leave to rise in a warm place until it doubles in bulk. Then roll out to half finger-thickness and cut into 8–10 cm (3–4 inch) squares. At one edge of each square place a spoonful of plum jam, roll up the square, dip in melted butter and place on a greased baking tin. Let the buns rise for another 10 minutes, then brush them with beaten egg or hot butter. Bake in a warm oven until golden brown.

83 Dumplings
(plum or apricot)

For the dumplings:
800 g (1¾ lb) potatoes
approx. 200 g (7 oz) flour
1 tbsp margarine
salt

For the filling:
600 g (20 oz) plums or apricots
*sugar cubes (as many cubes as you
   have dumplings)*
150 g (5 oz) breadcrumbs
100 g (3½–4 oz) butter or margarine
castor sugar
cinnamon

Dumplings

Cook the potatoes in their skins in salted water, peel and mash while hot. When cool, knead together with the flour, the margarine, the egg and a pinch of salt. Roll out the dough to the thickness of your little finger on a board sprinkled with flour, and cut into 5–6 cm squares. Place a stoned plum or half an apricot in the middle of each square, replacing the kernel with a sugar cube dipped in cinnamon. Flour the palms of your hands and shape the filled squares into dumplings. Drop them into boiling salted water and cook for about five minutes, until they rise to the surface. Drain, and roll the dumplings in breadcrumbs fried golden brown in butter. Sprinkle with castor sugar mixed with cinnamon and serve immediately.

84 Cottage cheese noodles

400 g (14 oz) flour
3 eggs
1 tsp cooking oil
300 g (10–11 oz) cottage cheese
100 g (3½–4 oz) smoked bacon
200 ml (⅓ pt) sour cream
salt

Cottage cheese noodles

Mix the flour, the eggs, a pinch of salt and a little cold water. Knead into a dough. Roll thin on a board sprinkled with flour, leave to dry and then tear into fairly large pieces. Cook in boiling salted water with one tsp oil added. Dice the bacon, fry, remove the cracklings, and set aside. Toss the well-drained pasta in the bacon fat, sprinkle with the sour cream, crumble the cottage cheese over the top and sprinkle with the cracklings. Before serving, place under a grill or in a hot oven to heat the sour cream and the cottage cheese.

85 Golden yeast-cake
(with wine sauce)

---

300 g (10–11 oz) flour
4 eggs
200–300 ml (⅓–½ pt) milk
20 g (¾ oz) yeast
150 g (5 oz) butter
200 g (7 oz) ground walnuts
4 tbsp castor sugar
1 tbsp rum
salt
1 tbsp icing sugar

For the wine sauce:
600 ml (1 pt) wine
60 g (2¼ oz) castor sugar
2 eggs

Proceed as for the bun dough (see page 66), that is to say knead a soft dough out of the 4 eggs, the liquefied yeast, the flour, 1 tbsp sugar, salt, rum, lukewarm milk, and 2 tbsp melted butter. Dredge with flour, cover with a clean cloth and leave in a warm place to rise. Now turn out onto a floured pastry board, roll out to finger-thickness and cut out 2 cm (1 inch) diameter rounds with a pastry cutter. Butter a fairly deep fireproof dish, dust with ground walnuts and dip the rounds of dough in melted butter. Arrange them in rows in the dish, close to each other, and sprinkle with a mixture of ground walnuts and sugar. Repeat this as you add further layers on top of each other. Put in a warm place and leave to rise once more. Brush the top with melted butter and bake in a moderate oven. Serve with wine sauce.

How to make wine sauce:

Whisk together the sugar and the egg yolk, add the wine and continue whisking while slowly heating to boiling point. Do not allow to boil. When the sauce thickens, add the whisked egg white, and continue to whisk with an egg-beater over low heat for another 1–2 minutes. Serve immediately while warm.

86 Cobbler's delight

For the noodles:
250 g (8–9 oz) flour
2 eggs
a little butter
salt
or 200 g (7 oz) ready-prepared thin
  noodles

For the filling:
150 g (5 oz) castor sugar
20 g (¾ oz) vanilla flavoured sugar
80 g (3 oz) butter
3 eggs
400 g (14 oz) cottage cheese
400 ml (¾ pt) sour cream
40 g (1½ oz) raisins
grated lemon peel
2 packets of rétes pastry (you need
  6 sheets altogether)
50 g (2 oz) butter

Mix together the flour, eggs, salt and a little water. Knead until you obtain a rather firm dough. Shape it into a lump, butter it and let it rest for half an hour. Now roll it out thin and cut it into thin noodles. Boil the noodles in plenty of slightly salt water into which you have added a little butter. Drain and add to the filling prepared as follows: whisk together the sugar, the vanilla flavoured sugar, the butter and the egg yolks. Add the cottage cheese rubbed through a sieve, the sour cream, the raisins soaked in water or rum, and the grated lemon peel. Mix well together. Finally, fold in the beaten egg whites. Butter a baking tin and line it with three layers of prepared *rétes* pastry. Spread on the cottage cheese and noodle mixture, and cover with another three layers of *rétes* pastry. Sprinkle with melted butter and bake in a moderate oven until crisp (20–25 minutes). Cut it up only after it has been out of the oven for fifteen to twenty minutes. Before serving, dust with vanilla flavoured sugar if you wish.

87 Pastry horn
(a Transylvanian speciality)

300 g (10–11 oz) flour
100 g (3½–4 oz) butter
200 ml (⅓ pt) milk
10 g (⅓ oz) yeast
5 egg yolks
2 egg whites
3 tbsp castor sugar
20 g (¾ oz) vanilla sugar
120 g (4 oz) icing sugar
150 g (5 oz) ground walnuts
lemon
rum
salt

Crumble the butter and the flour together on a pastry board, add the yeast liquefied in lukewarm milk. Mix in the egg yolks, castor sugar, salt, grated lemon peel and rum. Knead well, adding lukewarm milk, if necessary, until you obtain a medium-stiff dough. Shape into a roll, place it on a floured pastry board, cover with a clean cloth and leave in a warm place to rise. When it has doubled in bulk, cut it into strips ½ cm (¼ inch) thick and 2 cm (1 inch) wide. Then butter a fairly thick rolling-pin, wind the pastry strips round so that the edges of the strips butt up against each other. Brush with egg white and sprinkle with coarsely chopped walnuts mixed with sugar. Bake on a slowly revolving spit until golden brown, brushing it occasionally with a feather dipped in melted butter. When done, remove the pastry from the spit and dust with vanilla sugar. Serve hot. This pastry used to be made at fairs—baked over charcoal.

88 Cherry tart

For the pastry:
250 g (8–9 oz) flour
120 g (4 oz) butter
50 g (2 oz) ground walnuts or
*   almonds*
80 g (3 oz) castor sugar
3 egg yolks
1 kg (2¼ lb) cherries
grated lemon peel
sweet sponge cake crumbs

For the vanilla cream:
150 g (5 oz) castor sugar
50 g (2 oz) flour

Pastry horn (a Transylvanian speciality) ▶

4 egg yolks plus 2 egg whites
500 ml (1 pt) milk
50 g (2 oz) vanilla flavoured sugar
sweet sponge cake crumbs

Crumble together 250 g (8–9 oz) flour and 120 g (4 oz) butter. Mix in the ground walnuts, egg yolks, sugar, and grated lemon peel. Knead well and leave to stand in a cool place. Roll out to a thickness of about half a centimetre, place in a baking tin and bake in a moderate oven. Now sprinkle on sponge cake crumbs and tip the cherries (stoned and strained) over them.

For the vanilla cream:

Stir together 120 g (4 oz) sugar and 4 egg yolks, add the flour, then gradually the milk, and flavour with vanilla sugar. Bring to the boil and allow to thicken. Then fold in the egg whites beaten together with 30 g (1 oz) sugar. Spread the cream over the cherries, dust with sponge cake crumbs and put back in a moderate oven for about 20 minutes.

You can prepare this tart from morello cherries also, in which case you should use rather more sugar.

89 Poppy-seed and walnut rolls

For the pastry:
1 kg (2¼ lb) flour
500 g (18 oz) butter
30 g (1 oz) yeast
8 egg yolks
60 g (2½ oz) castor sugar
salt
400 ml (¾ pt) milk
2 eggs (for brushing over)

Walnut filling:
Bring to the boil 200 ml (⅓ pt) milk

mixed with 300 g (10–11 oz) sugar.
Pour on it the ground
walnuts (300 g [10–11 oz]), add
raisins, ground cinnamon, grated
lemon peel, 1 grated apple, and
mix together well.

Poppy-seed filling:
Bring to the boil 200 ml (⅓ pt) water
mixed with 250 g (8–9 oz) sugar,
pour it over the 300 g (11 oz)
ground poppy-seed, and mix with
grated lemon peel, 2 grated apples,
ground cinnamon, ground cloves,
raisins, and a little apricot jam
(add honey and rum too, if you
wish).

Crumble together the flour, the sugar, a pinch of salt, the eggs and the butter and add the yeast liquefied in a little milk. Now add the rest of the milk after warming it gently, and knead until you obtain a medium-stiff dough. (Knead well, until the dough stops sticking to your hands.) Cover it with a clean cloth, leave to stand for 10 minutes in a warm place, then shape it into 6 equal-sized balls. Roll them out into thin rectangles. Spread them evenly with the walnut or poppy-seed filling, roll them up, and place on a buttered baking tin. Prick them here and there over the top and take care not to place the rolls too close to each other as they will swell during the baking. Brush them over several times with beaten egg (first lengthwise, then crosswise) and bake in a moderate oven. They are best if you leave them to stand for 2–3 days. They are served traditionally at Christmas and Easter.

Poppy-seed and walnut rolls ▶

90 Strudels *(rétes)*
(apple, morello cherry, cabbage, or poppy-seed)

Since the frozen-food counters are full of prepared, rolled and packed *rétes* pastry, home-made *rétes* pastry is out of fashion these days.

Carefully place the prepared *rétes* pastry on a cloth dusted with flour (use two sheets of pastry placed one on top of the other for one strudel) and sprinkle with melted butter or oil (or a milk-and-rum mixture). Dust with bread—or cakecrumbs, and spread the filling over one third of the surface. With the help of the cloth, roll up the strudel, place it in a greased baking tray and brush with egg, melted butter or oil. Bake in a hot oven till crisp and golden brown.

Fillings for two strudels:
Apple filling:
1 kg (2¼ lb) apple
100 g (3½–4 oz) castor sugar
30 g (1 oz) walnuts
50 g (2 oz) raisins
ground cinnamon

Peel, core and thinly slice or grate the apple. Spread it over the prepared pastry sheets and dust with sugar mixed with cinnamon. Sprinkle raisins (soaked in water or rum and strained) and coarsely chopped walnuts over the top.

Cottage cheese filling:
400 g (14 oz) cottage cheese
3 eggs
50 g (2 oz) raisins
100–200 ml (4–7 fl oz) sour cream
150 g (5 oz) castor sugar
grated peel of half a lemon

Whisk together the egg yolks and the sugar. Add the cottage cheese after passing it through a sieve, then also add the sour cream, grated lemon peel and the raisins soaked in water. Finally add the whisked egg white.

Morello cherry (or cherry) filling:
800 g (1¾ lb) morello cherries (or cherries)
150 g (2 oz) walnuts (according to taste)
ground cinnamon
sweet sponge cake crumbs

Stone and drain the morello cherries and mix them with the ground walnuts and the sugar mixed with cinnamon. Spread the *rétes* pastry sheets with the sponge cake crumbs before adding the morello cherry filling.

Cabbage filling:
800 g (1¾ lb) cabbage
2 tbsp cooking oil
ground pepper
salt
1 tsp sugar

Shred the cabbage, sprinkle with salt and leave for half an hour. Squeeze out the moisture, add the sugar and fry in the oil. Season with ground black pepper, and when cool, use it to fill the *rétes* pastry.

Poppy-seed filling:
250 g (8–9 oz) ground poppy-seed
100 ml (⅕ pt) milk
1 large apple, grated
50 g (2 oz) raisins soaked in rum
200 g (7 oz) castor sugar
grated lemon peel
ground cinnamon
crushed cloves

Boil the poppy-seed in sweetened milk, remove from the heat, and mix with the other ingredients.

91 Apple tart

For the pastry:
400 g (14 oz) flour
1 egg
150 g (5 oz) butter
10 g (⅓ oz) yeast
2 sugar cubes
milk
salt

For the filling:
1 kg (2¼ lb) apples
100 g (3½–4 oz) castor sugar
50 g (2 oz) ground walnuts
1 pinch ground cinnamon
sweet sponge cake crumbs
grated lemon peel
1 egg

Strudels *(rétes)* ▶

Add the sugar and the yeast to 50 ml (2 fl oz) lukewarm water. Beat together with the flour, egg, butter, a pinch of salt and enough warm milk to produce a medium-stiff dough. Knead well, cover with a cloth and leave to rise in a warm place. Divide the dough into two and roll the two halves out. Place one sheet on a greased baking tin dusted with flour, and sprinkle it with sponge cake crumbs. Peel, core and grate the apples, and mix with the sugar, cinnamon, ground walnuts and grated lemon peel. Spread over the pastry sprinkled with cake crumbs. Cover with the other sheet of pastry, and prick with a fork. Brush with beaten egg and bake in a moderate oven until golden brown. Cut when cool.

92 Rákóczi cheese tart

For the pastry:
180 g (6 oz) flour
120 g (4 oz) butter
6 g (2 oz) castor sugar
100 ml (4 fl oz) sour cream
2 egg yolks
10 g (⅓ oz) yeast

For the filling:
100 g (3½–4 oz) castor sugar
10 g (⅓ oz) vanilla flavoured sugar
3 egg yolks
500 g (18 oz) cottage cheese
200 ml (7 fl oz) sour cream
30 g (1 oz) raisins
grated lemon peel
sweet sponge cake crumbs
3 egg whites
70 g (3 oz) castor sugar
apricot jam

Knead together the ingredients for the pastry and let the dough rest for at least half an hour. Roll it out to ½ cm (¼ inch) thickness. Use it to line a greased baking tin, prick it with a fork, and bake in a medium oven till half-done.

Blend the ingredients for the filling. First beat the egg yolks with the sugar, then add the cottage cheese after passing it through a sieve. Stir in the raisins (soaked in water and drained), together with the grated lemon peel and sour cream. Finally, fold in the stiffly beaten egg whites.

Sprinkle sponge cake crumbs over the pastry which you have already half baked. Spread the filling on top, and continue baking in a medium oven. When almost done, pipe the stiffly beaten egg whites and sugar in a lattice pattern over the top and continue baking until light brown. Fill the apertures between the lattice with apricot jam, and allow the tart to cool a little before cutting it into squares with a wet knife.

93 Pastry fritters

400 g (14 oz) flour
100 g (3½–4 oz) butter
20 g (¾ oz) castor sugar
half a lemon
50 ml (2 fl oz) rum
100 ml (4 fl oz) sour cream
4 egg yolks
salt
apricot jam
100 g (3½–4 oz) castor sugar
*   flavoured with vanilla*
oil for frying

Mix together the castor sugar and the flour. Add a pinch of salt, crumble in the butter, and stir in the 4 egg yolks, rum, sour cream, and enough lemon juice to produce a medium-stiff dough. Let it rest for about half an hour. Roll out to 2–3 mm ($\frac{1}{10}$ inch) thickness and cut into 15–20 cm (7–8 inch) squares. Use a pastry cutter to score parallel slits in 2–3 places. Pull the edges of the squares through the slits, knot them, then fry in hot oil until crisp and golden brown. Sprinkle with vanilla sugar and serve with hot apricot jam, which you can flavour with a dash of apricot brandy if you wish.

94 Vanilla cream tart

One packet deep-frozen puff pastry
500 g (18 oz)

For the cream:
200 g (7 oz) castor sugar
4 eggs
50 g (2 oz) flour
½ l (1 pt) of milk
a vanilla pod, or 50 g (2 oz) castor
sugar flavoured with vanilla

Thaw out the puff pastry and roll out into two equal sheets of about 3 cm (1 inch) thickness. Put on a greased baking tray and prick with a fork. Bake in a hot oven until golden yellow. Cut one of the sheets into 5×5 cm squares.

Meanwhile, mix the sugar, flour and one third of the milk together until smooth, then add the egg yolks. Bring the remaining milk and the vanilla pod to the boil. Add to the egg mixture and, stirring continuously, cook over boiling water until it thickens. Whisk together the egg whites and a little sugar. Add one quarter of this to the cream and continue stirring until smooth. Remove from heat, and add the remaining whisked egg whites. Spread the cream evenly over one

sheet of pastry. Cover with the squares cut from the other sheet and press them down gently. Now use a wet knife to cut through the bottom sheet also, along the line of the squares. Serve chilled, dusted with vanilla sugar.

95 Filled pancakes

For the batter:
2 eggs
250 g (8–9 oz) flour
200 ml (7 fl oz) milk, soda water
salt
oil for frying

Mix the ingredients and add a quantity of soda water to produce a thick, smooth batter. Let it rest for at least an hour. Heat a little oil in a frying pan with a handle. Pour a small ladleful of batter evenly over the pan, and fry on both sides. The pancakes may be filled with ground walnuts or almonds mixed with sugar, cocoa powder mixed with sugar, jam, cottage cheese mixed with raisins, a mixture of sugar and egg yolk, poppy-seed, chestnut cream, vanilla cream, and so on.

96 Gundel pancakes

For the batter: *see above*

For the filling:
70 g (3 oz) raisins soaked in rum
100 g (3½–4 oz) ground walnuts
70 g (3 oz) castor sugar

Prepare the pancake batter in the usual way. Fill each pancake with the sugar-raisin-walnut mixture. Fold in flour, arrange so that they overlap each other in an ovenproof dish. Pour on a rum and chocolate sauce and heat in the oven. You may serve them flambé if you wish, that is, with rum poured over the top and lit.

For the rum and chocolate sauce:

Stir together 100 g (3½–4 oz) sugar, 3 egg yolks and 1 tbsp flour. Thin gradually with 100 g (3½–4 oz) melted chocolate and half a litre (1 pt) boiling milk flavoured with a little vanilla. Cook over boiling water, stirring continuously until the mixture thickens into a cream. Remove from the heat and add 100 ml (4 fl oz) of fresh cream and a little rum to taste.

97 Slipped pancakes

For the batter:
300 g (10–11 oz) flour
60 g (2½ oz) butter
60 g (2½ oz) castor sugar
3 eggs
½ l (1 pt) milk
salt
butter or oil for frying

For the filling:
50 g (2 oz) ground walnuts
50 g (2 oz) castor sugar
30 g (1 oz) cocoa powder
50 g (2 oz) castor sugar

Cream the butter with the sugar. Blend with the egg yolks, a pinch of salt and the flour. Gradually beat in the milk as you do so. Finally, fold in the stiffly beaten egg whites. Make the pancakes a little thicker than usual but only fry on one side. Now slip them onto a fireproof dish with the uncooked side upwards, and dredge each one with the fillings (ground walnuts mixed with sugar, or cocoa powder mixed with sugar). Alternate the fillings until the last pancake, which you should place on top with the fried side upwards. Heat them up in a medium oven, but do not cook.

98 Walnut cake

For the cake mixture:
6 eggs
150 g (5 oz) castor sugar
180 g (6 oz) ground walnuts
100 g (3½–4 oz) flour
salt

For the cream:
80 g (3 oz) ground walnuts
80 g (3 oz) castor sugar
100 g (3½–4 oz) butter

Beat the egg whites until stiff with a pinch of salt. Carefully fold in the yolks, the castor sugar, the ground walnuts and the flour. Pour the mixture carefully into a greased and floured cake tin, put into a pre-heated oven and bake at a moderate heat for about 30 minutes.

Boil the sugar and the ground walnuts in 50 ml (2 fl oz) water. Remove from the heat, and mix in 100 g (3½–4 oz) butter. Let the mixture cool, then beat until white and creamy. When the cake is cool, cut it into two layers with a sharp knife. Fill the layers with the cream, spreading it over the top and the sides of the cake. Dust the sides with ground walnuts, decorate the top with walnut halves and chill.

Slipped pancakes ▶

99 Deák cake

150 g (5 oz) castor sugar
100 g (3½–4 oz) butter
100 g (3½–4 oz) almonds peeled
  and ground
100 g (3½–4 oz) flour
8 egg whites
chocolate cream (see page 80)

Cream the butter with 100 g (3½–4 oz) sugar. Fold in the egg whites whisked together with the remaining sugar. Add the ground almonds and the flour, and blend thoroughly. Pour the mixture into a greased cake tin dusted with flour, and bake in a moderate oven. When the cake has cooled, cut it into three layers. Fill them with the chocolate cream, chill, and pour melted chocolate on top.

100 Dobos cake

6 eggs
140 g (5 oz) castor sugar
140 g (5 oz) flour
2 tbsp butter (if you prefer a richer mixture)

For the top caramel layer:
150 g (5 oz) castor sugar

For the sponge cake:
Beat together 100 g (3½–4 oz) sugar and the egg yolks. Add the flour and continue beating until smooth. Six layers are required for the cake, so the mixture should be divided into 6 equal parts. Grease and flour the baking tins and bake the sponge cakes in a medium hot oven until pale yellow. Remove from the tins with the aid of a knife. Put aside one sponge layer, and fill the others evenly with the chocolate cream, spreading it over the top and the sides. Chill. Melt 150 g (5 oz) sugar in a saucepan, stirring with a wooden spoon. When the sugar is smooth and golden in colour, pour it over the remaining sponge cake layer and spread evenly with a knife dipped in butter. Immediately after spreading the caramel, take the buttered knife and mark out the caramel into 12 slices. Place the marked layer on top of the other five. Use a knife dipped in warm water to cut the cake.

For the chocolate cream:
Beat together 200 g (7 oz) soft butter and 150 g (5 oz) vanilla sugar until creamy. Boil 150 g (5 oz) chocolate in a little milk and sugar. Stir until smooth and thick, cool, add to the creamed butter and sugar, and stir thoroughly.

This cake acquired its name from its creator, József C. Dobos, a confectioner at the turn of the century.

Dobos cake ▶

AFTERWORD

*T*his is a selection of the most popular Hungarian recipes, both old and new. You will find a description of dishes served both in luxurious restaurants and in roadside inns and which are, in addition, firm favourites with most Hungarian housewives. Menus usually begin with a lengthy list of soups, since in Hungary soups are almost always the rule before meat dishes. In this way the appetisers are pushed into second place. Frequent accompaniments to meat dishes are the salads, which are rarely eaten here as a separate course. The desserts which end the meals, and which include custard, poppy-seed, walnut, chocolate, or cheese fillings leave hardly any room in one's stomach.

The reader will find detailed descriptions of, and recipes for, a number of basic and frequently occurring items of Hungarian cuisine, such as the various stews, paprika dishes, *tokány*s and goulashes. To begin with, we should point out that the *gulyás* (goulash) known the world over has not much in common with the traditional Hungarian dish containing beef and potatoes cut into cubes and stewed in a thick paprika and onion sauce. A considerably thinner version of this is the goulash soup with noodles. The beef, veal and pork stews consist of meat cut into cubes and stewed in a thick paprika and onion sauce, while in *paprikás* the sauce is made a little thinner, and then enriched with sour or double cream mixed with a little flour. The *tokány*s consist of strips of meat stewed with onions and other vegetables, in some cases with mushrooms and pieces of sausage.

As is well known, the traditional Hungarian cuisine is filling and rich in calories. However, in this cookery book we have tried to offer a variety of recipes which, while remaining fully authentic, will hopefully cause no health problems. That is to say, the taste of the food has been left unchanged but the proportions of fat, onion, flour, spices and pork have been adjusted in accordance with modern dietary require-ments. If, for health reasons, the housewife or cook uses oil instead of the lard or rendered bacon fat which is traditional in Hungarian dishes, the taste will be practi-cally the same. Nevertheless, in certain cases the use of sour cream or genuine Hungarian paprika powder is indispensable, as are good Hungarian wines to accom-pany the meal.

The recipes are given for four and can be undertaken anywhere in the world provided the quantities of the ingredients and the processes of preparation are observed.

Good cooking and *bon appétit*

Printed in Hungary, 1991
KOSSUTH Printing House, Budapest